THE BIG PRESENT IN THE BATHROOM

Lessons in Upside and Downside

Permanent Equity CIO

Tim Hanson

Illustrations
Sarah George-Waterfield

BORING BOOKS

Cover By: Sarah George-Waterfield
Illustrated By: Sarah George-Waterfield

ISBN: 978-0-9980300-8-1 (Paperback)
Printed in United States of America
First printing 2025

Published by Boring Books, LLC
315 N. Tenth Street
Columbia, MO 65201

CONTENTS

PREFACE

It came to my attention the other day that the people I office with (shoutout Holly, Taylor, Emily, Danny, and Joe) write down things that I say in earnest that they find amusing. So it went when I was trying to help Kelie update a financial model a third party had built for her and may have uttered something along the lines of "As with most spreadsheets created by other people, I don't know what's going on here."

I didn't mean it like that!

The point was that there are a lot of tools in the Excel toolbox and different people have different favorite functions so sometimes it's hard to reverse engineer what's going on in a cell or a formula and why someone coded something up the way they did. Yes, I know I need to get a life.

I can't blame them though because, as you'll see, I do the same thing with them and the things I write down (that I can also write about in a public forum…though Emily and I don't always agree on what should be shared publicly) often become the basis for these Unqualified Opinions and even titles of books like this one (sorry not sorry).

Because at the end of the day we here at Permanent Equity strive to keep you entertained and informed, and I hope this fourth collection of Unqualified Opinions does just that. And know that it wouldn't be in your hands if not for Holly's heroic efforts in the bathroom.

CAPITAL

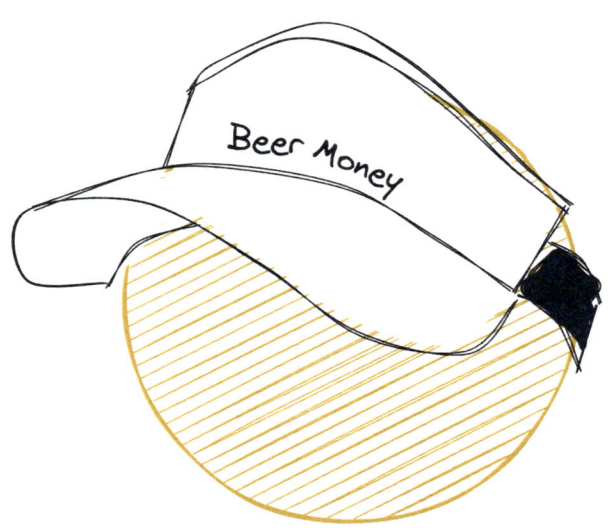

Beer Money

UNFAIR VALUE

Why returns are hard.

If you're in the business of investing, your product is returns, which is to say that if you're in the business of investing, returns are what your customer expects. But unlike other products, to the chagrin of customers and proprietors alike in this space, returns can't be manufactured at scale on an assembly line according to a production schedule. In fact, by trying to manufacture returns, investors often do worse (and/or commit fraud).

Yet if you don't have a product that you can reliably manufacture at scale and on schedule, you arguably don't have a business. And since I'm in the business of investing, I was some combination of outraged, amused, impressed, bewildered, skeptical, and cynical when I read about Hamilton Lane, a fund that reported that on one investment of pretty good size they made 39% in a day. And further that they had done stuff like that before.

The trick is that Hamilton Lane went into the secondary market for illiquid private investments and bought something for a price no one else would pay. Then they marked the value of that investment on their own balance sheet not at what they paid (or cost, as the nerds would say), but at a higher "fair value" (which is even nerdier) with "fair value" being what other people who owned shares in that investment thought it was worth.

Of course, people who own things have every interest in portraying them as worth more. An opposing force is that buyers have an interest in acquiring those things at a price that is less. What's the truth? Who knows?

Because arguably Hamilton Lane shouldn't have marked the investment at the value others were carrying it at, but rather that the others all should have marked their investments to the value that Hamilton Lane *had just paid.*

But Hamilton Lane isn't the only one in this industry massaging returns by citing fair value. To wit, mammoth financial firm Blackstone's $59B real estate trust is kicking ass only if you are willing to give it credit for the "appraised values" of its investments. What are appraised values? They're numbers in spreadsheets, not numbers being offered by buyers.

Is this a problem? I think yes and no.

Returns are what you put in your pocket (hello, beer money!), but an important qualifier is that what you put in your pocket depends on *when* you decide to pocket it and *why*. In other words, if you buy or sell something, you may transact at fair value, but more likely you're not. Because the reason you're transacting is because the price is a lot more or a lot less. In Hamilton Lane's case, for example, they may have gotten a great deal (unfair value?) because the seller was distressed and they were the only ones who could wire it money that day and so maybe they were right to then mark it up?

This is why this stuff is confusing.

A better way to think about it is that there are two types of value: Spreadsheet Value, which is an academic estimate, and Real World Value, which is what a willing buyer would give you in cash today. And both numbers are worth acknowledging and knowing because rarely are they the same.

As for which one is "fair," that depends. And that's why returns are so hard to manufacture (absent, of course, fraud).

TIME AND MONEY

And problems and opportunities.

I was speaking with an investor the other day who wanted to learn a little more about Permanent Equity, and he asked me about roles and responsibilities. He wanted to know what all of the people on the team do and how we work together, with a particular interest in how our founder and CEO Brent and I interact.

I knew right then that this person was not (yet!) an Unqualified Opinions reader because he did not know about the four important roles ie, the person who generates opportunities to take risk, the person who decides what risk to take, the person who executes, and the person who measures and reports on the results. At Permanent Equity, Brent is first and foremost the person who generates opportunities for the firm and where I come in is helping decide which risks to pursue.

Of course, the thing about taking risk is that doing so can also create problems and because of opportunity cost something that has crystallized for me since I wrote about the four important roles two years ago is that not only is it my job to think about which risks to take, but also about which problems to solve and more importantly *how*.

See, as chief investment officer I am accountable for allocating the firm's capital. While that capital stack includes money, it also includes time since we are paying people to do good work. In other words, we have time and money to solve problems and pursue opportunities so which should we do and when?

A reality that has troubled us over the past 24 months is the self-diagnosis (and we've told this to our investors) that we've probably spent more time mitigating downside than pursuing upside in our work with our portfolio companies to the detriment of our returns. That's because, even though we all know that compounding upside is what generates long-term returns, when you're in the thick of it with a challenged investment, that situation will tend to get more of your attention than thinking about what an investment that is going well might do next.

It's in recognition of this that one framework I've begun toying around with is that when it comes to operations maybe we should aim almost exclusively to solve problems with *money* (i.e., outsource, settle, etc.) and pursue opportunities with *time*. Because if we approach it that way our people will definitionally be spending more time on upside than downside.

Now I recognize that trying to solve every problem with money is a slippery slope, and I certainly don't want to advertise to the world that we will settle any lawsuits brought against us. That said, I think there's a there here and I want to stress-test it.

Time &
Money &
Problems &
Opportunities.

I'M STILL NOT PISSED

Just frustrated. Right now.

You may remember the "not pissed" person who had identified a problem that we weren't in a position to solve. The takeaway was that this person was right, but not right *right now*. Because in a perfect world, we'd solve every apparent problem. But the world, as we all know, is not perfect. We have finite resources, trade-offs, opportunity costs, and oh-so-many other contexts, and that's why many problems can go unsolved for some period of time.

This reality came to light in another context again recently when I got a call from someone we know running a business he'd recently acquired. He had the opportunity to make an aggressive investment that he was pretty sure would pay off great. The context, though, was that the business was already mildly levered from the original transaction and he'd have to borrow more to fund this investment. While he was friendly with the bank and thought they'd play ball, the maturity on his line of credit was around the corner. The worry was that if he borrowed and made the investment and it didn't play out as he expected, the business might violate some covenants on the debt and the bank might non-renew the line of credit. This would put the business in the precarious position of now needing to do everything it could to get back into compliance and those efforts could be counterproductive with regards to helping the new investment pay off.

I told him I didn't think he should do it, which frustrated him (but he was "not pissed"). That's because he was "pretty sure" the investment would immediately start paying off great. Given that context, what was the move?

"Well, how pretty sure are you?" I needed to know.

"Pretty pretty sure," he said. "Like 75%."

"But not 100%."

"Not 100%, no. And there is a chance, due to circumstances outside of my control, that it could go really poorly."

"Ok," I said. "If it goes really poorly, are you betting the company?"

"No, not at all," he said. "But I would need time to recover."

And that was the key point. When we dove in there, he estimated that the business might need 9 months to get itself back onto really sound footing and that while it was doing that, it didn't need to be risk managing a concerned bank that might pull or change the terms of its funding. So where we landed was that while this was a good investment risk to take, it wasn't perhaps a good investment risk to take *right now*. From an order of operations standpoint, the path forward was to renew the line of credit and *then* take the investment risk. Then if the investment went poorly, the business would still have the time it needed to course correct before an outside actor could change its course.

This is a simplified example, but it's to demonstrate the point that when it comes to taking risk, timing matters. One aspect of that is asking are we prepared to take this risk? And I think that's pretty commonly done. But another is asking that if we take the risk and it goes poorly, will we have the time we need on the other side to recover? This, I think, is less common, but more important. Because if you have the time you need to recover, you may not need to be as prepared, which might lead to more risk and therefore potentially more reward.

YOU EFFING GUYS

What it means to be different.

Danny and his great head of hair walked into my office with a smile on his face the other day so I asked what was up? (Not that Danny is normally dour or anything. Rather, it was clear that something entertaining had just happened.)

"I was on the phone with someone I met at DealMAX, and it was the strangest conversation. He started off by asking what the [eff] we do and after I told him we buy businesses using 30 year funds with no debt, all he said was 'The [eff]?'"

Of course, that prompt made me perk up because if you're dropping f-bombs in casual conversation with a member of the Permanent Equity team there is a 100% chance you are going to get written about in this space.

While that was an awkward start to Danny's call, it got better from there because it turns out that this guy had had in his estimation more than 7,000 conversations with private equity firms over the course of his career. He said that he'd always make sure to ask what made the firm he was talking to different from all of the other firms and why someone would sell them something instead of to the other guy for any reason other than "more money."

"And you [effing] guys," the guy told Danny, "are the first ones I've ever talked to whose answer actually makes you different."

 That's what made Danny smile, and it made me smile, too. Because it's one thing to tell people you're different, but another thing entirely when people tell you you are.

QUESTIONABLE CAPITAL ALLOCATION DECISIONS

Make them?

I admitted recently that I'm cheap, so it might have seemed out of character to buy a scoreboard ad at Mizzou promoting Unqualified Opinions. After all, I wrote way back when that if Permanent Equity ever bought a Super Bowl ad, it would probably mean that Permanent Equity had lost sight of what made it Permanent Equity.

The point was and is that it's a privilege to be in a position to allocate capital, so if you find yourself in one, you should do it wisely.

But buying a scoreboard ad at Mizzou to promote Unqualified Opinions is a questionable capital allocation decision, at least when you look at it in a spreadsheet. That's because, since Unqualified Opinions isn't trying to convert you into any kind of paying relationship, the ROI on paying anything to acquire Unqualified Opinions subscribers isn't very good.

Why'd I do it?

Someone told me way back when to never borrow to buy a depreciating asset. And that's good advice. Another recommended saving aggressively, but also never holding cash in excess of what's needed for an emergency fund when there are appreciating assets one can buy instead (remember it's *time in* the market, not *timing* the market, that matters). And that also makes sense. But a third, acknowledging those two recommendations, advised me to think long and hard about how I might think about spending on memories and experiences within the context of that guidance.

In accounting, when it comes to spending, there are two kinds: expenses and expenditures. Expenses are things you pay for that you also consume in relatively short order and therefore provide minimal long-term benefit. These are deducted from revenue on the income statement in order to calculate profit. Your net worth typically goes down when you spend on an expense.

Expenditures, on the other hand, are things you pay for that become assets on your balance sheet because they are expected to provide value for a long period of time. Buying a home, for example, is most likely an expenditure. Your net worth typically stays the same or goes up when you make an expenditure.

So which is buying a scoreboard ad at Mizzou to promote Unqualified Opinions? Here's where context matters...

The opportunity to buy a scoreboard ad at Mizzou only arose because my son's swim team needed sponsors to help fund a meet they were hosting for 60-plus teams from across the state. Despite working hard to find some, they were falling short of the necessary number. And that makes sense because if you're a business viewing this as an expense rather than an expenditure, it's a questionable capital allocation decision.

For me, though, there was also the opportunity to help fund the valuable experience of the swim meet for my son as well as the chance to have the shared experience (with our content team) of creating a scoreboard ad with a dot in a spreadsheets hat floating in the pool in a flamingo inflatable. And that's a memory that will always make me laugh.

And what are valuable experiences and memories that will always make you laugh? Those are valuable assets to put on your balance sheet.

OPPORTUNITIES

THE BIG PRESENT IN THE BATHROOM

A lesson in downside.

One of the things that's happened as Permanent Equity has grown and we've spun off and staffed up our events business Scratchmade and recruiting team 10th Street Talent is that we've had to grow our real estate footprint. So whereas if you had come to visit us a few years ago you would have found us all crammed in at 315 North 10th Street in Columbia, Missouri, now you can find us spread out across 315, 305, and 307. In the course of doing that, our landlord (shoutout John and Tanner) did some beautiful renovations for us, particularly so at 305, which was once a motorcycle repair shop, but now very much looks the part of the office of a world-famous private equity firm.

Except for one detail that infuriated our CEO Brent: the trash can in the first floor bathroom. I don't know where we got it, but it was admittedly an inferior product. It was small and plastic, and it shifted whenever you stepped down on the pedal to open the lid.

"You guys have such a nice office," Brent would say when he stopped by (he offices at 315, but the investing team is over at 305), "except for the small, crappy trash can in the bathroom." Then he'd want to know when we were getting a new trash can. And my joke was that if we kept the small, crappy trash can at least he'd always have something to complain about when he stopped by rather than have to look for something new.

But after many months of this scene playing out near daily, Holly had had enough of the grousing and told Brent that she would go buy a new trash can for the bathroom.

"Great," Brent said. "Use your company card. You have an unlimited budget as long as you buy it at Target."

Now, I thought this was a pretty risky career move by Holly and told her so afterwards. She had put herself in charge of solving an inconsequential, but highly visible problem with nearly unlimited resources without establishing clear expectations or

KPIs. If she ended up doing anything short of procuring the world's greatest trash can, it would lead to endless ribbing. This is the classic capped upside, lots of downside scenario that we should all strive to avoid.

But it ended up even worse than you think. Because the next time Brent stopped by after Holly had procured a much larger new trash can (thigh high, tasteful) and put it in the bathroom, before he could say anything, Holly stood up out of her chair and said "Brent, I am so glad you're here. I left you a *big present* in the bathroom!"

As soon as she said it, you could see she wanted to take all the words back. But it was obviously too late for that. So we all went and did the only thing we could do, which was admire together the *big present* Holly had left for Brent in the bathroom.

This, of course, is precisely why we should avoid capped upside, lots of downside scenarios. Because no matter how much downside you foresee, it can always end up worse.

STUPID EXPENSIVE GOLDFISH

Rules are rules.

I heard a funny story recently from a mom who went into Petco to buy two goldfish for her kids after agreeing to do so. She found them (the goldfish, not the kids) in a tank near the back of the store selling for 29 cents each and asked a salesperson to bag them up.

But hold on, the salesperson said, do you have a tank for them at home?

No, the mom said. I was just going to grab a bowl on the way out and fill it up when I got there.

You can't do that, the salesperson said. You have to get a tank and then set it up, treat the water, and let it run for three days. After that, if you bring us a water sample and it passes muster, then you can buy the goldfish.

$125 later the mom had a tank and a filter, a collection of chemicals, a fake plant, a small castle and some gravel. Then, three days after that, after her water had passed muster, her kids had 58 cents worth of "stupid expensive goldfish."

What is going on here?

Observation one is about the power of commitment to influence our behavior (shoutout Cialdini). The mom agreed to get goldfish thinking the cost was de minimis, but still did so even after the cost of doing so rose exponentially. So be aware of what you commit to and under what circumstances, because most of us have a hard time walking those commitments back.

Observation two is that rules make things more expensive. If Petco didn't care about the well-being of their fish, this was a 58-cent transaction, but since they apparently do, it was a $125.58 three day slog. Is this a brilliant upsell (Petco *is* private equity owned)? Or do they truly care?

This is relevant because I've been thinking about the cost of rules a lot of late. See, Permanent Equity plans to begin experimenting heading into next year with something we never thought we would: boards of directors. The goal here is to regularly convene people with both inside and outside views of a business to discuss long-term objectives, report on progress towards achieving those objectives, and, to the extent that that business is or is not making progress, identify strategies that it might implement to improve performance. This sounds like basic blocking and tackling, and it's not to say that we weren't doing this, but absent rules around how and when to do it, we were probably doing it too irregularly and without all of the right people in the room as we've grown.

But board meetings are also *really expensive.* Not only does it take time to implement structure and abide by it, but the constraints imposed by objectives in and of themselves limit open-endedness. So we also don't want our boards to be like other boards. Our intention is to keep them small, highly accountable, and responsible for making sure each business has a clear plan, but for the cadence of collaborations underlying the process for achieving that not to be *regularly,* but rather *when necessary.*

Because if you do things because they have to be done and not

when they should be done, you end up with too onerous of a
regulatory regime...and stupid expensive goldfish.

REAL INTELLIGENCE

And the problems it solves.

We hosted our portfolio company leaders here in Columbia, Missouri, recently for our annual Operators Summit, and one of the discussions we had was around how we might better leverage technology to help make our (relatively) small businesses more efficient. It was then that I learned from Kevin, who runs our ridiculously cute and resoundingly fierce children's clothing company Rylee + Cru (I know the kids in your life need some additional style), that artificial intelligence (AI) was now handling some 40% of customer service inquiries and that that number had increased from just 10% in a few short months.

Someone else, listening in on the conversation, asked if his in-house customer service team, seeing this trend, feared for their jobs? But Kevin said no, that they loved the AI because it enabled them to spend more time solving the customer service inquiries that required depth of touch. And that I thought was an interesting observation.

 See, customer service is one of those domains where I think the barbell applies. In other words, there are very few medium customer service problems. Rather, there are small problems that are best handled quickly and complicated problems that are best handled carefully. Further, while handling the small problems quickly can show up almost immediately on the income statement in the form of revenue retention, it's handling the complicated problems carefully that can create tremendous lifetime value and turn your customers into zealots who will proselytize for your brand. Since we all want those, giving your real customer service people the capacity to do that is a big win!

 After all, AI is called artificial for a reason: it's not real (and it's still bad at math). So an interesting thing to think about is which problems in your business might require real intelligence.

For example, looking at the data, AI would have no problem identifying sales or margin shortfalls and even making recommendations, trained on data, on how to fix them. But what if the root of the problem was that one of your salespeople had developed an addiction or that someone on the finance team was stealing from the company? Those are real problems.

Having implemented our new boards of directors, I find myself sitting on the board of Scratchmade, our newly-named events company that was born out of all of the building we did to host Capital Camp and Main Street Summit. Clayton, who runs that operation, and I were talking the other day about how we might continue to grow that business, and I said that I was so long-term optimistic about the opportunity of an enterprise that seeks to deliver genuine, memorable experiences to people that make us more real and more human. After all, I said, trillions of dollars of capital have now accrued to businesses that make us less human, which is how I think of social media, so why wouldn't some percentage of that find the opportunities that do something so much more valuable?

Because in the end, that's my hope for AI. That it can take away from us the things we spend time on that make us less real and less human, so, like Rylee + Cru's customer service team, we can spend more time on the things that make us just that.

THE GOALIE IS SO STUPID

Or what if she isn't?

The u13 girls soccer team I help coach is on a run of success, recently winning a statewide tournament. In the course of doing so, our keeper saved (or forced misses) on five of the seven penalty kicks she faced (one in the course of play in the semifinal and four of the six she faced in the shootout that decided the championship). That's a remarkably good percentage, and it's my hope that I somehow contributed to that success.

See, one of the things that our keeper has started doing after she and I talked about how to be successful in penalty kick situations is not standing in the middle of the goal as all keepers do, but a step or two to one side. The objective in doing so is to turn the shooter into a forced actor. Because by making one side of the goal bigger than the other, it ostensibly makes the decision about which side to shoot at for them. This, I think, has two effects:

- If the side of the goal that's open is not the one the shooter typically likes to shoot at, it makes them uncomfortable; and
- It takes away about 40% of the goal that our keeper has to think about covering, so she only has to focus on diving one direction. And even though she can't get to the far post since she's not standing in the middle, because she only has one direction to dive, it takes a shot perfectly to the corner to beat her.

And it's really hard to, under pressure, place a shot perfectly in the corner. Funnily enough, as the shootout that decided the championship was getting started, the opposing team was standing near our bench watching our keeper prepare to save the first shot. Seeing our keeper line up, one of the girls on the other team remarked too loudly, "The goalie is so stupid. She's not even standing in the middle of the net."

Ha.

So remember two things. First, it's really hard to be successful if you get turned into a forced actor under pressure. Second, if it seems obvious that someone else is doing something stupid, maybe reexamine your assumptions before recommending further action. You may not be wrong, but at least consider the other possibilities.

SERENDIPITY NOW

What if Doug had unplugged that phone?

"How did you get here?" is an interesting question to ask and be asked. So it went on a recent call when a college student I'd been introduced to wanted to know – because I think he was interested in doing the same – how I had become the chief investment officer of a private equity firm.

"I," I said, "have a fairly non-traditional background, so take from this what you will..."

Coming from Long Island, N.Y., where I did landscaping as a summer job, I went to Georgetown University in Washington,

41

D.C., because I thought at the time I made that decision that I was interested and had a future in government. But I got an internship in the House of Representatives early on there and realized I had very little interest and definitely no future in government. I also found that I liked my political theory (shoutout Plato) classes far more than my practical politics classes because of the writing and thinking and so eventually wound my way to being an English major with a concentration in playwriting (which is why after I became CFO of Permanent Equity with no classical training in numbers, our CEO Brent would refer to me as the most under-qualified CFO in America).

I graduated from Georgetown in 2003, which wasn't a great time to be looking for a job what with the economy still recovering from the double shocks of the dot-com bubble burst and 9/11 (both formative events in my life that had occurred before the college student I was telling this tale to had even been born... ahem). Without a lot of prospects, I was expecting to head back to Long Island to landscape and then maybe go on to graduate school. In fact, I hadn't even received a response from any of the more professional jobs I had applied to, including one as a writer at The White House, which I had applied to at the recommendation of one of my English professors even though I didn't think I was qualified.

And I wasn't!

See, the job *required* a master's degree, and I didn't have one. Because of that, I later learned, my resume was put at the very bottom of the pile.

But never underestimate serendipity.

Because they interviewed everyone on top of me in that pile and none of them got the job. So the choice came down to interviewing unqualified me or reopening the process, which meant it might take six to nine months to fill the role. And so I ended up on the right side of the fact that something is better than nothing.

Now, an important thing to know here is that this happened a long time ago and I didn't yet have a cellphone. So the number on my resume was attached to the landline at the house I shared with a bunch of others on Potomac Street near campus. But by the time this all happened, we had graduated and were moving out. I kid you not that my roommate Doug was about to pull the jack out of the wall when the phone rang with The White House calling on the other side.

An interlude...

Getting a job writing at The White House might sound

impressive. You're probably thinking about memorable lines spoken during grandiose speeches on impressive stages. And there were people who did that.

But what also happens is that the President meets, greets, and receives gifts from a lot of people that then need thanking. And someone needs to write those thank you notes because the President doesn't have the time for that, but also wants to promptly send detailed thank yous because votes and also because not thanking a world leader for his or her gift might cause an international incident. Again, something is better than nothing.

And that's how I got hired for that job. Because I was better than nothing. But I'm still not close to telling you how I became the chief investment officer of a private equity firm...

That wheel started turning because I'm a cheapskate. Not as cheap as Morgan Housel (shoutout Morgan...we good?) and not as cheap as I used to be (shoutout past me), but always and still stingy. What's relevant is that back when I worked as a thank you note writer, I saved everything I could in order to be relentless about investing.

One reason I learned to be relentless about investing is because my Dad was relentless about investing. In fact, he started as a professor at SUNY Stony Brook (now Stony Brook University) around the same time as Jim Simons, the founder of the wildly successful quantitative investing firm Renaissance Technologies who recently passed away. Jim and my Dad shared a relentless interest in investing and allegedly talked shop, but Jim I think pursued that interest somewhat more relentlessly (if measured by financial outcomes and so it goes). That said, my Dad was still relatively relentless about the topic, and I took that in.

So as a young, relentless investor with a small amount of savings near Washington, DC, I inevitably happened upon The Motley Fool (based in Alexandria, VA). Then as I read The Motley Fool, I discovered that they were looking for a writer (and then ended up working there and doing other things).

I'm going to fast forward because this is getting long and attributing things to serendipity seems lazy, but I will say that another question I get asked is: "Should I work at a big company or a small one?" My answer is that big companies might pay you well and give you lots of training and small companies might pay you less and provide minimal training (and the government might…well, I won't comment on government jobs). You can do well anywhere, of course, but I think something about working at small companies is that you get the opportunity to do whatever you want. That creates variance and variance is upside (unless you screw it up). So if you value the future over the present, the opportunity to do more and earn less until later is always worth more (shoutout lifetime value) than the opportunity to do less and earn more in the present. Even a lot more (unless you screw it up).

Back to serendipity (and whoa is this too long a tale), I got hired at the Fool just as they were recovering from the dot-com bust, so I was a very junior employee at a very small company given the opportunity to do whatever I thought I should to add value while sitting at the same pod everyday as Bill Mann (you've met him before) and Fool co-founders David and Tom Gardner.

Serendipity.

I listened first-hand as smart people debated not only what investments to make, but also how to run a business that was at times under stress and at other times very much not. I guarantee you that the people being hired into Amazon or Apple or Goldman weren't and aren't being afforded the same opportunity.

After more than a decade of doing that (and a short stint managing Morgan), I got introduced to Brent Beshore (because of Morgan...it all comes full circle), saw what Brent and team were building here in mid-Missouri and thought it was pretty smart, and was paying attention when he told the world he needed someone "with a breadth of financial, accounting, and tax experience to help lead our team." Even though I had little of any of that, I sent him an email saying that I thought I could be helpful, we met, and here I am. So the answer to how I got to be the chief investment officer of a private equity firm is: I was curious. I learned from great people. I worked hard. I took risk. And I got lucky (because I don't think I ever applied for and then was offered a job I was qualified for).

And curiosity, mentorship, work, risk, and luck is a helluva equation. But I'll tell you, I often think what might have been different if Doug had unplugged that phone.

PEOPLE

NOT THE THUMBS UP!

LOL, right?

I learned the other day that Holly thought I was upset that her boyfriend parked in our lot on the day they went out to lunch together. Sure, we have finite spots, but it wasn't a big deal, so I asked her why she thought that.

"Because when I told you in Slack that he was doing that, you responded with a thumbs up."

An aside here about the thumbs up. I *love* the thumbs up. I think it's a universally positive and reassuring gesture. In fact, one of my favorite cities in the world is Sao Paulo, Brazil, because when you're driving there and you do something nice for someone, you get a thumbs up (and if you do something nasty, you get a thumbs down, which I also find delightful).

But apparently my view of the thumbs up is outdated!

So I looked into the matter and learned that Gen Z views the thumbs up as "actively hostile" and an unsettling "passive aggressive dig" and that it's rude to respond with one. Which is why Holly thought I was pissed. Then I thought about all of the people and things I had recently responded to with a thumbs up. One of those was a bunch of illustrations that SarahBethGDub had just finished and sent me for this whatever it is.

"Hey," I slacked. "Holly just let me know that the thumbs up is a rude passive-aggressive dig. I didn't mean it that way. I liked all of the drawings a lot."

"No problem," Sarah slacked back. "I've learned to translate it in my head."

But *then* I found out that if I didn't put an exclamation point (!) at the end of "I liked all of the drawings a lot" that Gen Z would view that as being a sarcastic comment.

WTF?!

Back when I wrote about seven reasons to sell, I heard back from an intermediary (shoutout Grant) who said that "by far the most common reason [business] owners want out is they can't deal with younger generations" and find them exhausting. I hadn't heard that as much and thought it was an overstatement at the time, but perhaps it's true.

It's important to say here that I don't find Holly exhausting LOL!! (If I end a sentence with LOL and multiple exclamation points I'm told that means it's heartfelt and genuine.) But I will say that generational differences are real and if not explored in good faith together can be impediments to the growth and development of an organization. (And they certainly shouldn't be the catalyst to you selling your business.)

Our friend Steve Cockram says that if you are going to lead an organization that employs members of Gen Z, then you need to become a leader that people want to follow. That means appreciating the contributions of others, apologizing when you need to, and appropriately supporting *and* challenging in order to get the best out of your team. Of course, that's good advice no matter who you find yourself leading, but it will only become more important as Gen Z takes on more and more senior roles in the workforce.

That said, I don't think I can ditch the thumbs up, but perhaps I can add a few more exclamation points to my emails LOL!!

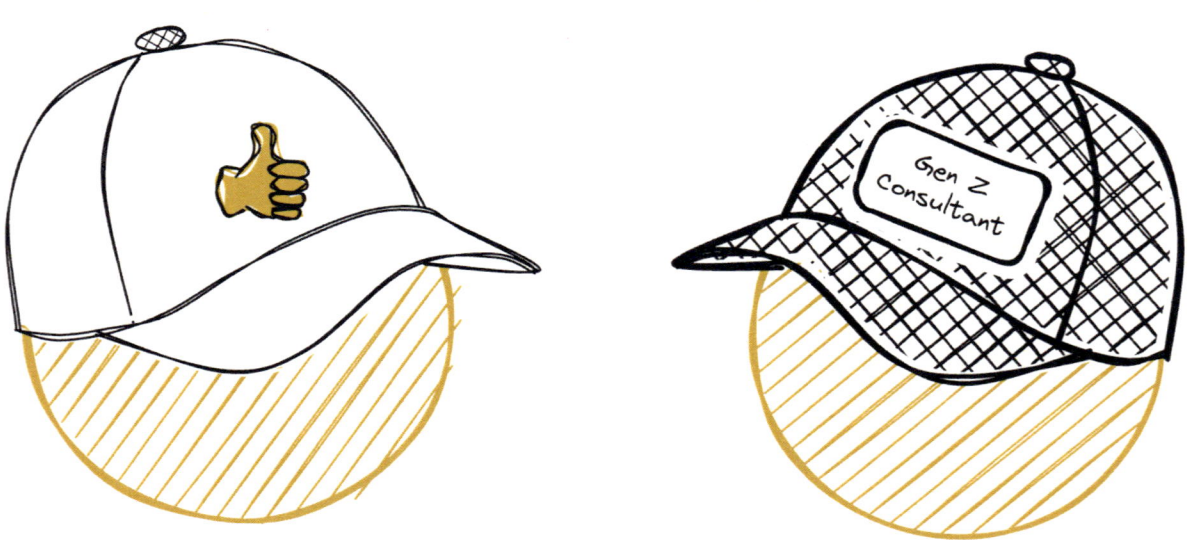

FUN IS IMPORTANT

Not everybody thinks so.

I was having lunch with someone who runs a small business and he asked me what I thought the biggest sign of a healthy business was. I rolled that around in my head while I took a bite of gyro (shoutout Beet Box) before saying, "I think it's if you can tell that the people who work there are having fun."

Before you call me corny, hear me out. Because here are some things that are probably also true if the people who work at a business are having fun:

- They want to be there.
- They have genuine relationships with customers, suppliers, and coworkers.
- They know the objective.

- They are having success.
- They are optimistic about the future.
- They feel appreciated.

If you have a business with fairly-compensated engaged employees getting after the plan, that's a healthy enterprise. And the inverse, a business with under- or over-compensated, disengaged employees who don't know the plan, definitely isn't.

Of course, if you had told a younger version of myself that fun was the most important KPI, I would have scoffed. So I've come a long way.

At this point, I'll reveal that I've had that beginning to this whatever-it-is written for a while now, but hadn't followed through on finishing it because I thought the takeaway seemed a little light and not important enough to tell you about (not unlike a previous one of these that was deemed not my best). And I continued to think that until John Linehan, President of Irresistible Foods Group (parent of King's Hawaiian among other brands), dropped by our office wearing a floral print shirt to visit the other day and started telling us about their Grillo's Pickles business.

Grillo's, he said, was his favorite business to visit. The reason that was so is because the energy in the building is infectious. From the minute you walk in the door, you, like everyone else in the building, feel all in on solving pickle problems (and he told us about some doozies involving exploding pickle pallets at Costco). And that's because they're having fun solving fun problems with fun people. And while that fun has begotten growth, he said if the growth ever came at the expense of fun, he would sooner give up the growth.

"Not everyone thinks this way, but I believe that if you're not having fun doing what you do," John said before leaving, "you should do something else."

Well, I think that way too. Now, at least. And it's important enough that I tell you about it.

BUSSIN'

Or pretty mid?

I was bewildered to discover that Gen Z views the thumbs up as "actively hostile" and an unsettling "passive aggressive dig." What's more, this came not long after I read that Gen Alpha considers something "weird, cringey or random" Ohio (though my daughter tells me that no one uses that term any longer). So imagine my delight when I saw Hyundai's new Internet Dad spot.

In it, a middle-aged man asks his daughters how they are feeling about the pancakes he's griddled only to be told that they're "pretty mid" (which is what kids these days call something that's not good). He responds by breaking out a litany of modern slang (aura…flex…bussin') to his daughters' horror and dismay.

Somewhat related, one of the most important parts of our diligence process is getting to understand the specific terminology a business uses to describe itself. This is because, without that knowledge, it's often impossible to understand what a business is doing, why, or how well. For example, lots of businesses "nurture qualified leads," but what makes a lead qualified and how it is nurtured can vary widely from company to company. But even more so than that, just like Hyundai's Internet Dad, people can also often use words in weird ways.

See, back when our managing editor SarahGW was working to make our comprehensive diligence checklist fit for public consumption, one of the observations she made was that it seemed like we were often asking the same question over and over. For example, when it comes to risk assessment, among other things, we'd like to know:

- What debt do you have?
- What do you owe to someone else?
- Do you have any obligations to repay someone in the future?
- Have you promised to give anyone money in the future in any way?

And yes, these do all sound like pretty much the same question.

But if you were to ask our very thorough chief legal officer Taylor why we do this he would tell you that it's because if we don't get very, very specific, we're likely to miss something. Because here are some real things we've heard in response to those aforementioned questions:

- "That's not debt. That's just a loan I gave the company."
- "Oh, I only have to pay that if I ever have the money."
- "I mean, I told them that they'd get a bonus if I ever sold the company, but they're not expecting anything."

Bussin'.

OH NO!

The risk of not doing what you think you're doing.

At the risk of oversharing, there are two – and only two – things about me that endeared me to my wife and caused her to marry me:

1. During a freshman year art history class in college I surprised her by being able to speak at length about the significance of contrapposto in classical sculpture.
2. When I tell a story that I think is seriously funny, I crack up laughing and can't get through it.

And we'll be married 20 years this October. So there you go. As for what stories crack me up, here is one of my favorites...

Back in another life I managed money invested in emerging

markets. This meant I got to travel quite a bit with my friend and mentor Bill Mann, which was the best part of the job. Bill, despite being a veteran traveler, could occasionally be absent-minded, and that's how we found ourselves in Santiago, Chile, with Bill needing to get pages added to his passport so there was room in it for him to be stamped back into the U.S. upon our return. He dutifully made an appointment at our embassy there to do so and we had a tight window for me to drop him off in the rental car and then get to our next meeting.

As we all know, you can't park anywhere close to a U.S. Embassy, so I dropped him off and then told him I'd wait across the way in the parking lot of a service station. I did that, but after about 20 minutes the attendant came over and tapped on my window and politely told me to get the eff out of there because I wasn't a paying customer. I acquiesced to his request and therefore started circling the embassy hoping to be passing by when Bill came out. And it was maybe on my tenth or twelfth loop on the *Avenida Andres Bello* that I saw Bill emerge from the embassy, walk across the way to the service station, and inexplicably get into a different car.

What the eff is he doing? I thought. But then I went around the bend and lost sight of him.

When I came back around the other side I pulled into the service station and saw Bill standing there looking sheepish. I slowed down; he hopped in and told me to drive.

"Did you get into that other car?" I asked.

He had, he said. He thought it was the same gray sedan as our rental and since he was rushing to get to our next meeting he had blindly opened the door, sat down in the passenger seat, and commanded his new amigo to drive.

That's when an elderly Chilean man, fearful that he was being carjacked by a six-foot-four American, stared at Bill with wide eyes and bellowed "Oh no!" (and this is where I usually crack up telling the story and can't get through it).

Bill, realizing his mistake, slowly exited the car with his hands up and then waited awkwardly in the lot until I swung back around to pick him up with the elderly Chilean man eyeing his new amigo suspiciously the whole time.

The reason I'm telling this story now, aside from the fact that I enjoy telling it, is because something nearly identical happened to me just the other day. There I was sitting in my car outside of the Mizzou Aquatic Center waiting to pick my son up from swim practice. It was freezing out (a recurring theme this winter) so people were rushing to their rides. I had my head down checking emails on my phone when the passenger door opened and a strange kid burst in and told me it was time to go.

"You're not my son," I stammered, hoping I wasn't about to get mugged.

That's when the kid (I later found out it was Luke) looked up from his phone and said "My mom has the same car!" Then my actual son rushed up and asked Luke what he was doing in his seat. Luke, some combination of mortified and confused, said again that his mom had the same car and scurried off looking for her.

So then I had to tell my son the "Bill Man Oh No" story on the way home...and couldn't get through it without cracking up.

 All of that is to say that we tend to make a lot of unexamined assumptions when we're in a rush and that those assumptions can expose us to a lot of risk – "Oh No!" risk, let's call it. So even if you're in a rush and it seems inefficient, try to always take the minute to make sure you're doing what you think you're doing.

SURPRISES ARE FUN

Here's how to have them.

When you get to be my age it's not often that you are finding and/or creating new favorites any more. I know what I like and I've seen a lot, so there aren't too many surprises. Which I admit is sad, because surprises are fun. That said, I completely unexpectedly experienced my favorite soccer moment ever recently and so I have to tell you about it...

The context here is that every winter the now u13 girls play in a futsal tournament called the SuperCup and every winter we lose in the final to a team from Springfield. This year looked to be no different when we lost again to them in pool play. While we did win enough games in the opening rounds to earn a rematch in the final, expectations were low because our goalie and another starter couldn't be there and another player had to sit out with a broken foot. In fact, we almost forfeited because it looked like we wouldn't even have enough players to play. But we cobbled together numbers and another player volunteered to play in goal despite having limited experience doing so. Suffice it to say that Vegas hadn't installed us as favorites.

In the huddle after the warm up but before the game I said, "Guys, I know we're nervous. But let's just take this chance to have fun and get better. And if we get [the goalie] out of here without a broken nose from getting hit in the face with the ball, let's call that success."

That made them smile.

"So be attentive. Match their energy and effort. And stay in front and block their shots to set [the goalie] up for success." Then we talked about switching formations to play man-to-man defense for the entire game, which is a big ask from an effort standpoint, but was the system that would give us the best shot at being competitive.

The game started and we promptly scored to go up 1-0. Big smiles. But then we did have a few inevitable miscues near our goal and the half ended with us losing 1-3. Yet we were in the game working hard and having fun.

The second half started and the girls' effort level went through the roof. The other team couldn't get through or around us, and we were blocking shots or forcing shots from distance that our goalie with *limited* experience – to her immense credit for stepping up – handled. Then we scored off a corner. 2-3.

I called timeout to give them a rest and said, "Keep it up. Also, their goalie is off her line so if you get a chance to shoot from distance, take it."

The game resumed and we got a steal. Our player took a dribble forward and then unleashed an inswinger from mid-court that beat the goalie, deflecting in off of the bottom of the crossbar. Tie game. What a shot. Wow. The gym was loud and there were about five minutes left. The ref comes over to tell both coaches that if the game ends in a tie, there will be a five-minute sudden death overtime followed by penalty kicks if *that* ends in a tie.

A minute later one of our defenders stepped forward and intercepted a pass their goalie was trying to make. She slammed it in. 4-3 and holy cow.

Now the other team called timeout and changed formations to chase a goal, which they ended up scoring with 20 seconds to go. But we were still having fun. Then the overtime went by with no goals so the game was headed to PKs – and us with a goalie with *limited* experience.

If you were around last season, then you know that I have spent *a lot of time* thinking about PKs in the context of soccer, but also life and work. They keys to success are to:

- Have a repeatable process.
- Don't be a forced actor.
- Prepare for stress.

The vibe in the huddle was incredibly positive. One of the girls made a joke about the goalie breaking her nose and another expressed mock outrage at another for losing the game of rock paper scissors that decided who got to pick who shot first. So we didn't seem stressed. I picked our shooting order and told the goalie to just make herself as big as possible and trust her instincts. Then I was surprised to learn from the referee that we would be shooting first. Despite winning rock paper scissors the team from Springfield decided to shoot second.

Now, there's some conventional wisdom out there that shooting second is the smart choice because then the shooter knows for sure what she needs to do. But I don't think knowing what you need to do has any impact on skill or effort, but instead serves to increase stress. And since most PK misses are not saved, but rather shots that miss the net, doing anything to increase stress on your shooter is a dicey proposition.

In the first round, we made ours and then our goalie with *limited* experience saved theirs. We're up 1-0. Then both teams made it. Then we missed and they made. Then both teams made it. So it's 3-3 and coming down the last round. Our player stepped up and made it. Their player stepped up knowing she absolutely had to make the kick or lose...not looking like she was having much fun...and slammed her shot off the post.

I don't mean to keep holding up a u13 girls soccer team as a teaching tool for life and work, but I love this story and think it illustrates a few simple things you can do to create massive competitive advantages:

- Show up (we didn't forfeit).
- Work hard (if the effort is there, the results will follow).
- Set others up for success (and your own will take care of itself)
- Have fun (and enjoy the people you work with).

Do that and surprising things can result. And surprises are fun.

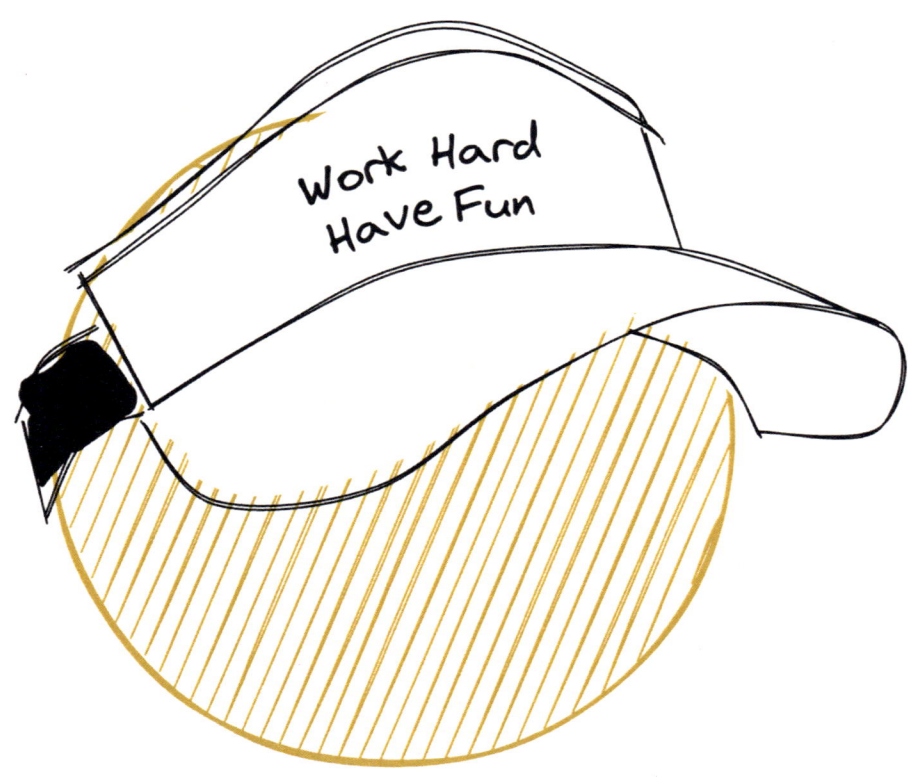

ABOUT THE FIRM

Permanent Equity invests in private companies deliberately built for long-term success. We commit for the long-haul with 30-year funds, no intention of selling, and rarely use debt.

With Permanent Equity, what happens next doesn't have to be concerning or complicated. When we invest, "next" means that we serve and support, build meaningful relationships, and roll up our sleeves to preserve legacy and grow without goals. There's no 90-day plan, no harm, and no assholes.

If you care what happens next for your company, your employees, your customers, and your family, we invite you to read and listen, and, when you're ready, reach out.

ABOUT THE AUTHOR

Tim joined Permanent Equity in 2018 and now leads the firm's Investing team. He also works closely with its Operating team and leaders at portfolio companies to help make decisions about capital allocation. Outside work, Tim enjoys running, gardening, and soccer-ing.